LONE WOLF THEORY

A guide for people who don't have a pack

Luke Balleza

LONE WOLF THEORY

Copyright © 2022 by Luke Balleza

All rights reserved. This book or any portion thereof may not be reproduced or used in any manner whatsoever without the express written permission of the publisher except for the use of brief quotations in a book review.

Contents

Chapter One: The Lone Wolf 1

Chapter Two: Being Abandoned by the Pack 21

Chapter Three: Alpha vs. Sigma, Choosing to be Alone 43

Chapter Four: Time Alone 65

Chapter Five: Fighting Your Own Battles 83

Chapter Six: Making the Best of What You Have 97

Chapter Seven: Being Ok With Being Alone 115

"Abandoning the pack also means leaving behind the protection other members offer. Because of wolves' territorial nature, loners must be cautious about trespassing into lands belonging to other packs. To safely find food, a lone wolf may need to search for hundreds of miles. Or, a wolf may float between the borders of pack territories, checking scent marks to make sure that it isn't in danger. To further conceal its whereabouts, a lone wolf limits its howling because it could give away its location to enemies [source: Mech and Boitani]. The exception is if a wolf accidentally gets lost from the pack -- it will howl to signal its location" [source: Feldhamer et al.].

CHAPTER ONE

The Lone Wolf

Wolves have been depicted in our scriptures and art as far back as man can remember. It's as if they're as old as time itself. These beasts have been found in stories, drawings, carvings, and artifacts from every corner of the world. In some cultures, the wolf is revered as a mysterious and elegant spiritual being with powers beyond our physical realm.

On the other hand, some cultures display these creatures as violent beasts ready to stalk you down

Lone Wolf Theory

and slay you in cold blood. Regardless, these animals have fascinated humans for thousands of years, creating an endless amount of folklore and campfire stories.

Humans were so close to these animals that we even domesticated them and inbred them until we got the domestic dogs that we know today. Our dogs in our homes can't even compare to the elegant but savage nature of these beasts. God blessed these animals with amazing features, such as their ability to see in the dark and their super-fast speed of up to 35 Miles per hour. Alongside sharp teeth with bone-crushing jaw power and an amazing sense of smell like a great white smelling blood.

In their natural habitat, the wolf breed as a whole is a pure example of a family in the animal kingdom. Mainstream biology knows that these predators instinctively thrive on daily contact with their own species. They have developed their own form of communication and hierarchy amongst themselves. Social interaction and communication are the backbones of their community. They depend on this community and protection of one another to sustain life in their remote environments.

Just like best friends or a close-knit family, they have each other's backs. Having a solid back up and support increases their chance of survival in their harsh environments. Years of evolution are hardwired into these animals. Therefore, they understand that having reinforcements is their lifeline and safety net for any member of the pack.

If a wolf is lost, it can howl back to the pack and be found. If a wolf is hurt, the pack protects the injured wolf. Every member of the pack is required

Lone Wolf Theory

to help with the birth of the pups. When it's time to eat, they hunt together in unison, with each one playing a role in taking down large prey such as elk, deer, and moose. Their power in numbers leads to great success in their hunt. Moving together, wolves act militantly as they form ranks in preparation to flank. Meeting back together after a kill, they leave with full stomachs moving together as a single unit.

Over the years, scientists noticed an odd behavior that began to occur within the pack life. Based on long-term observation and study, they noticed that ever so often, a wolf is banished from the pack or chooses to leave the pack, forcing itself to fend for itself. In the animal kingdom, this is better known as the Lone Wolf Theory.

The term lone wolf comes from a blatant mental behavior of a select few wolves among a pack. Most are aware of the deadly repercussions of being alone. Wolves are known to be apex predators in biology, meaning that they are predators that do not get hunted. In other words, they are on top of the food chain, and there is no one to take them down. This does not mean that they are immune to death. They are also living organisms that need to maintain their bodies to stay alive.

Just like humans, they form a totem pole of order. The alpha wolf is the king and the shot caller that leads the way and breeds with a majority of the females. He is respected and has earned that position by being a fearless warrior and also defends it with pride when tested by younger males. The alpha calls the shots and picks and chooses who gets to stay with the pack.

The alpha keeps the pack in order. He knows that the pack ensures the survival of its fellow

Lone Wolf Theory

members through harsh, cold, and desolate conditions. He is on top, but he knows that without each other, members die off, but with the power of numbers, they are helped.

Like brothers in arms, no one gets left behind. There have been stories of wolves dragging their wounded to safety or even going after hunters who shot and killed wolves from their pack, circling them and howling. They heavily count on one another, so they fight to the death and die with each other.

Scientists started to notice that once in a while, a wolf would just leave the pack on its own. This seemed to go against everything that was understood about wolves' behavior. Hence, they were amazed.

When they observed a lone wolf, they saw that it would never return and that once it left, the wolf ran away for good, hunting and surviving on its own until it found another pack that would accept them. Or they would just accept their fate. They would just die due to the fact that the chance of survival on their own was so slim. It's as if these wolves felt like being in a family setting with their pack was not ideal for them or their future. They would, therefore, literally rather live on their own with so much pride that even in the face of death, they would not return.

The fact that some go rouge is absolute suicide, but they clash to match with the alpha pack leaders to live in peace. And the wolves who are outcasted are thrown away for not being able to provide. Against all odds, both are forced to fight for their lives all on their own. The wolves either venture from the pack by choice due to the way they are treated by pack members or lose their mating partner. The ones who are banished from the pack

Lone Wolf Theory

are kicked out for not pulling their weight or for being poor hunters.

Regardless of their loss of a family, they're on their own. Their chances of life are slim, every single move must be cold and calculated, or else they're dead. There is no one to catch their slip-ups. They're against the world now with no help or support when times get hard. Their will to survive is a true testament to the mental and physical power of this animal.

Wolves are wild animals, and on top of having animal instincts, they are predators with a pack of backup. This gives them more of an advantage over other animals, making them sit higher up on the food chain. Their will to survive in harsh conditions is wired into the very core of their DNA, even if they find themselves on their own.

The Lone Wolf

What about humans, though? Some people are blessed with loving, caring families who gather around the dinner table and invested in each other's interests and days. Their relatives believe in "family over everything." People have beautiful relationships that lead to lifetime marriages with support. Others have close and dear friends who will loan them their last 20$ and even pick them up in the middle of the night with short notice. There are even people who have all three: Friends, family, and a spouse. They have love and support from all three angles of love in their life. But what about the forgotten ones... The lone wolves.

Not everyone is born with equal opportunity or support. There is a simple but famous saying we all have heard "Life is not fair." We live in a world where children are abused and abandoned. Some kids get

Lone Wolf Theory

outcasted by others, leaving them with no friends or support groups. Also, unfortunately, people's wives or husbands leave them. Sometimes someone can even lose their whole family to circumstances they cannot control, like a car accident or fire, and their entire lifestyle suddenly changes.

Whatever the case, some people are forced to carry on alone with no family, no friends, and no support. They're on their own. They are the human version of a lone wolf, living life with the pure definition of loneliness. It takes a toll on anyone who has to take this journey alone.

So, what does one do when life kicks them in the balls? Do they give up and give in or stand their ground and push back? Fight or flight is an understatement when you're fighting tooth and nail to see another day. Life is cold and unforgiving at times, so without a doubt, we need a support group.

The Lone Wolf

We need pure and genuine love when things are simply not going our way.

Just like wolves, we seek a "pack." We, humans, need some sort of family/friend group to rely on. Having people in your corner softens the blows when things are not going out the way it's supposed to. Plus, having people around you is almost like medicine.

We all have days, weeks, and even months when life knocks us down. Having a support group helps us spiritually, physically, and mentally when we feel like we want to give up and not wanting to live. It's in our human nature to rely on each other when times are tough. People act as our invisible safety net.

Have you ever had a horrible day, and someone close to you talked to you or went out of their way to help you? All of a sudden, you instantly feel better, like a weight has been lifted off your shoulder and that things will eventually be ok no matter how down you're feeling. Having simple, supportive human connections with positive interactions can make a drastic difference in our whole way of thinking. It can even make the difference between someone calming down to see the bigger picture before making a rash decision with negative consequences.

We all have made horrible choices that we end up regretting down the road. Learning how to think before acting requires a tremendous amount of self-control and maturity. Unfortunately, many of us are walking this path alone, as I have been stressing in this book. Having no one requires tremendous internal strength that requires you to have the will to carry on and keep yourself in line.

The Lone Wolf

You're the one who has to put yourself in check because no one else will do it for you. This is a challenge, especially when you are on your own. Being forced to sit with your thoughts can be a burden, especially when they are negative.

The thoughts you don't speak but are in the back of your head are always the truth. They are a reflection of how you feel, even if you're embarrassed to share it with anyone else. Thinking to yourself simply means you are telling yourself the truth. In this mindset, there is no one to impress, so these thoughts are the complete and ugly truth of your reality. You sit there dwelling on them, and as they marinate intense feelings, they begin to surface. Raw emotions are a mother fucker. They will eat you alive or fuel your drive.

I've seen loneliness as it affects hundreds of people in my life, both positively and negatively. We

Lone Wolf Theory

live on an enormous planet, and a majority of us will never be able to see every corner of our planet in our lifetime. Once you grasp this concept, you start to understand how different our lives can be compared to others. We all come from different cultures ,households, and circumstances. These directly affect how people react differently to being on their own. It either motivates them to keep surviving and fighting their way out of their situation, or it's an excuse to waste away their lives by just blaming the world for what happened to them and refusing to change anything about their situation.

We are more familiar with loneliness being a negativity of life. I mean, no one wants to feel alone. It's a shitty feeling. From the outside, we mainly see the reaction of self-destruction and apathy toward the human experience we call life. Loneliness is a quiet cancer that plagues the minds of millions.

There's a cure, but what if I told you it's not from a pill? It only comes from within yourself, but most people don't want to get cured. They end up crashing and burning.

Like I keep saying, life isn't easy, and its core comes down to survival of the fittest. You either get back up, or you're a one-man army. Some go through it with the support of others, and others have to push through by themselves. Either way, it's a bitch. And this bitch is unpredictable. She'll love you one day and then hate you the next.

Sure, you can take the easy way out and do something drastic, like ruin or end your life, but a majority of humans have the will to survive. People have survived the most horrific circumstances. War, famine, fatal injuries, and even being lost at sea. Even if they feel like dying, the human body will attempt to carry on against all odds. Making it to see another day is hardwired into our brains from thousands of years of fighting to live.

When those dark thoughts come into our minds, most people can calm them and silence them. We won't go on a shooting spree or end our lives. But no matter what, we can't deny the depression that comes with being on our own and having to stand tall in the face of adversity. We're humans, and we are connected to this world until we are gone. We must wake up every day and put one foot in front of the other to make it through. That makes us special, unlike a rock or piece of wood. We adapt. Relying on ourselves and others is how we make it. So please start to understand how this affects us when someone has no one to lean on.

People react differently to these circumstances, almost like a fight or flight response. I can give two

The Lone Wolf

examples right now of one of the wealthiest icons known today and one of the most notorious and evil faces remembered from the not-so-distant past. One might motivate you while the other one might make you sick, but what do they both have in common? They both had to be lone wolves growing up with absolutely nothing. They both were born in poverty with no support or guidance. One made it while the other self-destructed. It's amazing how once you see how their reactions were, it's like night and day.

My examples are the pure definition of polar opposites, Charles Manson and Oprah Winfrey. We must question what the effects of true loneliness are on an individual. Will you become a successful individual with the ability to be resilient or a homeless strung-out career criminal?

I picked these two because it's a powerful testament to the point that I am trying to get across in this book. Some of us are forced to fight and survive on our own. I guess the question is will loneliness turn you into a stronger and wiser person? Will it help you handle situations that others can't? Or will it destroy your outlook on life and bring you to your knees?

I was alone for the majority of my whole life because of the terrible choices I made as a teenager and young adult. I wrote this book to help you understand that I have been alone too. I woke up alone, and I went to bed alone. For the longest time, I did everything on my own. I have cried myself to sleep and been full of rage. I know what it feels like to spend birthdays and Christmas holidays alone or to be left by the love of your life. I have been betrayed by my best of friends. I have felt the shame of my own mother wanting nothing to do with me. I know what it's like to feel completely alone. It's a feeling that everyone will not experience to the degree that I and many others have. It will make or break you. This book is to help you navigate through life alone without sinking your ship. I pray this book restores your faith and spark the fire that will bring light to the darkness around you. We are lone wolfs, never forget that. Surviving alone made us fiercer and more resilient than the rest. Stand in your power.

CHAPTER TWO

Being Abandoned by the Pack

"To be rejected by someone doesn't mean you should also reject yourself or that you should think of yourself as a lesser person. It doesn't mean that nobody will ever love you anymore. Remember that only one person has rejected you at the moment, and it only hurt so much because to you, that person's opinion symbolized the opinion of the whole world, of God."

– Jocelyn Soriano

We never remember what it was like to be a

baby or a toddler. It's almost like a blur filled in from stories and pictures from others. What we do know is that our mind is still developing and adapting to the new world we have entered. But one thing is for sure, no one comes into this world wanting to be abandoned. Most of us don't want to abandon our loved ones, even when we are upset with them.

The Human experience is full of happiness as it is full of pain. Struggling with the pains that come with being alive burdens us all. We confine in love to get through the pains together. However, some people lack empathy and don't have that emotional bond with their loved ones. These people are able to disconnect from close connections, cut ties and get up and leave with no rhyme or reason. Being abandoned and rejected is extremely painful when we want that person to stay with us.

Being Abandoned by the Pack

When you're a baby or a toddler, you want to be picked up, nurtured, and loved, even though you do not fully understand the emotions related to love. Babies can't explain love at that age because it is impossible for them. However, for some reason, babies instinctively know what love feels like and the comfort and warmth it provides. The want for love and affection is carved deep into our neuropathways.

If you really sit there and think about family, love, and birth, you will notice that no one can be born without at least their mother present at their birth. Most of us in the developed world cannot imagine someone abandoning a child without at least giving it up for adoption or to child services. But unfortunately, this happens way too often. People can even get abandoned simply by friends and family not supporting or being there for them when they are needed for a shoulder to cry on or a crutch to keep on moving.

To get deeper on this, people actually get abandoned at all ages. When this occurs, humans act comparably to the wolf pack. When their pack abandons them, the weak sink and the strong float, it is survival of the fittest. At this point, we now know that The Lone wolf is the wolf that is all alone with a greater chance of dying. They have the hardest chance of survival because now they have to fend for themselves. Some prevail or find a new pack but others give up and ultimately die off.

People seem to have a similar reaction when their pack gives up on them. Being left out by our friends, family, and lovers can be some of the most painful experiences in our life. The betrayal and

Being Abandoned by the Pack

anger tied to being let down are indescribable. It feels like we're thrown away like a piece of trash on the side of the road. There was no real explanation or valid reasoning for their actions. This hurts, especially when it's done by those who were supposed to support you. This choice that they took crushes your soul and pins you down. You sit there confused and say, how could this be? How could they go? The sad part is that no matter how hard you think and reflect on it, there is no good reason why they left you. They were supposed to be there for you until the end. A loss like this is overwhelming when it's from the ones you were truly relying on.

Being ghosted like this stirs up some of the darkest emotions the human body can feel, mix that with the hardships of your life, and you create hate, anger, and resentment. At this rate, it's easy to build a grudge and a fuck it attitude. I mean, why not? You were left behind in a ditch! Now you're cold. You have no love and support because the people who were supposed to provide it didn't step up. You were thrown away like a piece of trash, forced to pick up the pieces of your life on your own. Of course, you're going to not give a fuck.

Everyone can think of a friend or person whose parents were not there for them. The effect it has on them almost always shows up negatively in some form. They start to get in trouble, fight, start getting into drugs, etc. They are the forgotten ones. The children of the corn.

My main point is that they start to act out against life and go against the grain. They start to self-destruct and erode. Being abandoned by anyone who we humans put on a pedestal has major effects on our whole psyche. Look at a common wone like having an absent father for example. We all know

Being Abandoned by the Pack

that a father's job is to teach you how to be tough, take care of your family, and protect the ones you love. Or what about not having a mother whose job is to teach you how to love, nurture, and care for her family? Even not having friends affects the ability to have people to open up to share thoughts, ideas, and opinions or to rely on when things get hard. Or being left by your lover, not feeling loved, or even being in a relationship hurts so many people who want to have a life partner to raise a family with or start a household with.

These people we admire are what we consider our tribe. Our tribe is our community that defines our purpose. People who get left by their tribe are truly lonely people. They are lonely because they lack the love that others take for granted. Love comes in all forms. Unfortunately, some of us don't get to experience the love that others receive.

Lone Wolf Theory

Knowing what I know now has made me respect everyone's pain. I'm very mindful of what others struggle with, and sometimes, we cannot tell how someone truly feels. I understand why it stings deep into your heart when you are left behind. But use it as a chance to reflect on yourself to see if you were part of the problem as well. Acceptance and admitting is the first step in being free from the pain.

The problem that comes with holding on to the resentment of being abandoned is that the person most likely isn't thinking about you if they did that. Blaming someone who was not there for you gets you no further from where you were yesterday. I see people blame their fathers or mothers for their problems. It's an excuse, and a means to act out for attention, like I said. They will never admit that they're wrong. They end up always searching for the love that left them.

Being Abandoned by the Pack

In third world-countries, there are stories of babies who were left in a field abandoned by their mother because their mother was a young teen who was raped or just too poor to take care of the child, so they leave them in a field to die. I know this is the most extreme example of being abandoned by family, but this shit is real, and abandonment comes in all forms. Like the bitter man who treats women like shit because the one he really loved walked out on him. He struggles to find that love again, so he takes it out on women because that's what hurts him.

No matter what form abandonment shows up in, we all know that it greatly affects who we become and how we act in our early teens or adulthood. The sad thing is that we can only control our actions at the end of the day. It does not matter how much we want people to stay in our lives. Humans come and go. We cannot control what they do or what happens to them. Eventually, we have to accept what has happened, or we'll never take our power back.

Taking your power back and standing in it is liberating. It can only happen when you're able to accept what has been done to you. You're able to remember the pain, but somehow, you do not let it consume you. When you take your power back' you will be able to get out of bed. You will stop crying, stop wasting your life, and you will start to make the necessary moves to be happy again.

Staying bitter and closed-minded shuts the doors that could lead to finding a new pack and new opportunities. Being negative shuts down manifestation. Once we take our power back and accept the situation, we will start to manifest what we once lost, and we will be able to survive. Your power is what is going to push you and drive you to fix the circumstances given to us. People will feel bad, but

Being Abandoned by the Pack

the sad truth is that no one else is going to fix your life for you. Loneliness should motivate you to change. Change will make you fierce again. Being fierce on your own will help you survive until you find a way out.

There are some programs and guidance for children, but once you're in your late teens and adult years, you're left to your own devices. All you get from people is I am sorry or that's life. Think about this, people will adopt and orphan a dog, will crowd over the dog no matter what age they are, and they will get love and support it. Petting it, sleeping with it, feeding and caring for the dog, and also giving it the love that it craves and deserves.

What about humans? Once you reach about 16 to 18, you're on your own for the most part, even if you got abandoned by your people. At 18, you're a legal adult, and once you hit 21, you're expected to

Lone Wolf Theory

be in control of your life actions and responsible for changing them accordingly. If you murder someone, you go to prison, and if you don't pay your rent, you get evicted. This is the age we're expected to know the consequences of our actions and that we're responsible for controlling our situations or outcomes with or without help.

Sure, you'll meet people who will help you along the way, but chances are that you won't get the same love from the people that left you. And the older you get, the more and more you notice that no one cares. You're really on your own. Isn't that crazy that that's the type of world we really do live in, where adult dogs get taken care of and nurtured more than abandoned adults?

After seeing and experiencing being left, I noticed something that was a pattern. Being left and abandoned by the ones you love affects people in

Being Abandoned by the Pack

three ways. You may spend your whole life saying poor me while making it an excuse to live a shitty life, or you take it out on others by being an angry, bitter person, or it lights a fire under your ass, making you work extra hard, almost motivating you to change the outcome for your children or the people you find on the journey you started alone.

One of my favorite stories of someone who had been abandoned is the famous story of a homeless lady who became a lawyer. This lady literally went from the lowest level in our social society to becoming one of the most respected professions in our society. From eating out of trash cans to charging thousands of dollars an hour just a few years later. This is the pure definition of rags to riches. After knowing that this is possible, what could possibly be your excuse besides self-sabotage? If a homeless lady can become a lawyer and own her own law firm, then you can turn your life around too.

If you're worried about being a bad person and not being able to change, well guess what? Bad people really don't worry about changing their lives. All of our answers to our problems are buried within us and come out through our actions and behaviors. Having to go through life with loss and abandonment like this really fucking hurts in the moment. It stings to the very core of your heart. The safety net we once had and relied on is gone. The rug is ripped out on you before you even saw it coming, and now you're all alone, flat on your ass. But life goes on. And when life goes on, we need to survive. The world is unforgiving, and it doesn't care if you're all alone or if you have 4 siblings, 7 aunts and uncles, and 30 cousins.

We have to adapt to being alone, or we will not

make it through. We are humans, not wolves, but we still have similar survival instincts that let us adapt. Adapting to changes is one of the most amazing attributes we humans have. Humans have this amazing ability to survive against all odds and come out on top just by simply adapting to the changes they are forced to experience. It is the only way we can survive on our own. It acts almost like a coping mechanism when things change from what we are used to.

Look at the boy who was raised by wolves. When they found him, he was howling, eating raw meat, scratching, and biting like a wolf. People were terrified of him, and the story went all over the country. This was very odd for us to see, but if he did not adapt after being abandoned by his parents, he would not have survived in the wild with these wolves. It was so strange to see a boy scratching, howling, crawling, and eating raw meat. To us, this was insanity but it is a true story that has been passed down for years and can still be researched today due to the fact that it was well documented.

My real problem was that I never wanted to take accountability for my actions. I was a piece of shit in my early teens. I was truly out of control, wreaking havoc and hurting people with no care in the world. My attitude and way of life hurt the one person that I thought would always have my back.

My mother couldn't control me anymore for she had tried everything in her power to get me to wake up. She was convinced I was going to die or end up in jail. Her last resort was to give me tough love. She forced me to experience how cold and unforgiving the world is when you're truly forced to be on your own.

Being Abandoned by the Pack

One day my poor mother had enough and made me leave her house with no more help from her. I had to fend for myself. I was so mad, and I felt abandoned. I asked myself, how could my own mother do this? She abandoned her own son! I truly thought my hardships were caused by everyone's actions but not mine. I was so selfish. I finally understood the truth when it was too late.

If my mom had never abandoned me and gave me tough love, I would have never changed. Getting cut off taught me how to grow the fuck up and get shit done on my own. It taught me accountability and responsibility for the actions I made. I eventually made up with my mother and things smoothed over. That was until she got sick and passed away.

My mom left me again. But this time, it was for good. I pushed a lot of people away or people left me, but my mom would always pick up the phone

Lone Wolf Theory

and talk to me about anything. I got mad at God, mad at myself, mad at everyone. All it did was drive me insane because, you know what, my mom wasn't coming back, and I had no control over it.

I sat in a funk for a while after that and just started to go through the motions. Until I met a girl named Valery. She wasn't perfect, but she was perfect for me. She was the first professional, clean, and respectful woman I had dated. I really ended up falling in love with her, and I dated her. She started to help me heal slowly and look at what I was doing with my life. She helped me dress cleaner, talk cleaner, and want better in my life. She was the spark that helped me clean up my act.

One day she said one simple sentence that put me onto a whole different path and journey. She said, "your mom would want to see you do the right thing." These words left me dead in my tracks. It made me pause and take a real look at the bigger picture. These words motivated me so much that I cleaned up my act and became responsible. I took charge of what I had control over and started to change. When I changed, my life got easier and happier. It was like magic. I believe to this day that my mom and God sent Valery to me to open my eyes up.

I got tested one last time when things didn't work out between us. I became lustful, and she left me when I made the same mistake twice. I hurt her so much that I changed the way she looked at me. I was alone again. My lover had left me and wanted nothing to do with me. The woman that healed me and built me up was the same person that smashed my heart into pieces.

Lone Wolf Theory

I was in the same predicament again, and I was alone again. I had relied on something outside of myself for love. I was supposed to be finding that in my self so that I could add her love in addition to mine. This is the healthy thing to do when in a relationship because there will be fights and time apart. When you truly love yourself, you won't have to seek it out when they are not with you.

When Valery took her love back, I was flat on my face and heartbroken. She was the only friend that I really trusted at that time in my life, so it was really hard to let go and accept. I didn't listen, of course. I kept trying to talk to her, see her, give her gifts and show her that I really cared. I gave her all the love I possibly could, and it didn't work. I couldn't change her mind. It was too late now, the damage was done, and she was her own person. I couldn't make her stay because she was ready to go. She wanted to go her own way, and I tried to get her back because I was in fear of being alone.

It took a while, but I dug up what I learned from the relationship, and I healed again. That was the last time that disappointment from others almost led to my self-destruction. We have to move past it and accept it, or we won't survive on our own. Some people won't come back because what is done is done. How we react and handle the present moment will determine our future. That's all we can control. If you know you've done everything in your power, then accept that they are gone, pray and start to heal and let go. Everything is a lesson, whether they are good or bad. You need to take these experiences at face value and grow from them, or they will cripple you for the rest of your adult life.

CHAPTER THREE
Alpha vs. Sigma, Choosing to be Alone

"The person who follows the crowd will usually go no further than the crowd. The person who walks alone is likely to find himself in places no one has ever seen before."

– Albert Einstein

Wolves have 2 main types of personalities in the pack: the well-known alpha and beta. Every single animal shows the same personality types, including humans. Social

Alpha vs. Sigma, Choosing to be Alone

status defines everything from our money, power, respect, and who we can sexually attract.

The Alpha personality is the loud asshole at the bar, always trying to fight and compete to win the power and praise from women and weaker males. Power and status define their entire being. Then there is the poor beta scared to compete and stand up to the alpha. They easily fall into line and dare not compete in fear of embarrassment or loss. They act as pawns to kings or workers for a boss. They are the average Joes. Then there are the omegas, who tend to be at the bottom of the society. These include people like janitors or dishwashers.

What if I told you there is a fourth personality type? A personality that does not care to compete for status and power. They are rouge, choosing to live a lonely life, but they live it with pleasure. They walk through life, answering to no one. The ultimate bad ass while minding their own business at the same time.

This psychological phenomenon is known as the sigma personality type. It was not named the lone wolf personality type for no reason. Regardless, scientists and psychologists know that Alpha, Betas, and Omegas are the most common personalities.

Alpha wolves call the shots in the pack, and they are, without a doubt, the shot callers and leaders. When a beta or omega wolf doesn't pull their weight, they are thrown out with no questions asked. Lower-level lone wolves don't survive long in the wild, but once in a while, they pull through. Unlike Betas or Omegas, Sigma personalities choose to separate themselves from the social hierarchy simply because it burdens them to fight and cooperate with the

Alpha vs. Sigma, Choosing to be Alone

Alphas. The pack is an anchor to their freedom of choice so lone wolves separate themselves from the pack. Believing that the pack will slow them down and that they're better off surviving on their own is what justifies their actions.

Instead of fighting the leaders of the pack for control, they make a decision to fend for themselves. Sigma behavior is described as the superior personality type of a wolf that has been outcasted. Thus in the wild, they have the best chance of survival.

Just like wolves Sigma humans are very misunderstood but mysteriously intriguing people. The power they have discovered in isolation radiates off their bodies. They are aware that choosing to be alone comes from a deeper routed pain that Sigma hides.

Lone Wolf Theory

It's easier to take care of yourself than to deal with the emotional hurt that comes with being close to others. It's almost like not letting others into your heart guarantees no chance for them to hurt you or leave you.

I remember being younger and one of my mentors telling me something that would change my life's perspective forever. However, I wouldn't realize the truth in his words until later on in my life. He told me that I would be lucky to have 2 good friends I could count on and confide in. I thought that was a joke because I had so many friends and people loved me. I could call and hang out with so many different people. Little did I know that I would find out the hard truth later.

Being social in our young teens is a big part of a lot of our young lives. As a teenager, you take your

Alpha vs. Sigma, Choosing to be Alone

friends' opinions over your own parents' any day. I would even put more trust and time into my friends than anyone else. I would enjoy seeing them more than my own family. That all changed when they started acting differently toward me. I had a few times really embarrassed myself in school. Being that young, rumors and embarrassment will crush a young kid.

There was a time when I really needed nothing but my friends' support more than anything in the world. No one would stand up for me in fear of being getting dragged into the conflict. The torment got so much worse when the alphas decided to tease me publicly. No one wanted to stick up for me because they also did not want to get teased and embarrassed. My friends went with the temperature of the social situation and started to distance themselves from me.

I was left out in the cold because the alphas declared that was the cool thing to do. This was the first time I saw the reality of human nature; it showed me how people would present their true colors when socially pressured. From then on, nothing was the same. That was the day when I realized I could accept people's help and support, but at the end of the day, I could really only depend on myself.

I developed the sigma mindset. I started thinking like a lone wolf. Getting close to friends would weigh me down and lead to me being let down by them. So what is the point of getting close to anyone? It was easier to avoid it altogether. I found out that I could avoid a bond by setting boundaries before they got a chance to play with my emotions. I couldn't let

Alpha vs. Sigma, Choosing to be Alone

myself go through that again.

I started to just let people come in and out of my life as they pleased. I didn't hold any expectations of a friendship. I just gave people the rope and let them hang themselves with it. Realizing that humans show their true colors under pressure was eye-opening. If they fucked up, it was easier for us to go our separate ways.

I was still friendly with others, and I always will be. I just was done with having so many fake friends. I mean, it's not truly their fault because everyone is naturally selfish, and some people just have opposing views. My new outlook was a true awakening; it was the real beginning of my sigma behaviors. Being a sigma just made the most sense to me.

I experienced loss countless times by the time I was in my late teens. For this reason alone, I really started to be alone by choice. As I started to grow in

Lone Wolf Theory

life, I also was changing mentally, and I started to notice that I was different from most young teenagers my age. I didn't care to follow peer pressure, I could not be influenced easily, and if I did something, it was because I wanted to. No one could pressure me to be a certain way or act a certain way if I did not feel I should. My spirit was free.

I seemed to just stay in my own lane and do my own thing even if no one wanted to do it with me. I felt so free. I didn't need or seek anyone's approval or validation. Bullies tried to fuck with me, but I didn't feed into the games. This eventually stripped them of their power. Absolutely nothing could get to me. It eventually came to a point that I didn't care what my peers thought about me, whether it was positive or negative. I could not get embarrassed anymore as I did in the past. It was absolutely impossible to get to

Alpha vs. Sigma, Choosing to be Alone

me.

I retrained my brain, and there was no need or desire to roam with a crowd and have their acceptance. This was the point when I truly knew I was a sigma. Now that I think about it, even since I was a child, my friends would always ask me why I never wanted to follow along or why I wanted to do my own thing and not play with them. To me, it made no sense to them as to why I did not want to hang out. It's not that I didn't enjoy my friends; it's just that if I didn't believe in something, then I simply didn't want to do it. Why exhaust my time and energy when I don't even care if everyone else enjoyed it? I walked through life immune to social peer pressure.

I confidently say that I could survive on my own. I'm not encouraging you to be a loner because it is

Lone Wolf Theory

not healthy to limit friendships and interactions. But what do we do when the pack does not accept us for who we are, or what if they turn on us? Do we simply just give up? No! We're lone wolves, and we keep surviving even on our own. Even if that means we have a better chance of survival on our own.

I don't hate people who thrive on power and validation. It's natural for us to compete, especially for status, respect, and material gain. It has been going on since the beginning of time. War and conquest are in our DNA, and there hasn't been a period of time on this earth where there has not been in conflict and powershifts. We even measure success by status, wealth, and power.

Who doesn't want to be a king or an emperor with money, power, and respect? I'm a sigma at heart, and I'd rather be a warrior in the shadow than

Alpha vs. Sigma, Choosing to be Alone

a ruler of a kingdom. Sigmas are the assassins, ninjas, and silent killers who work alone. Powerful but mysterious and discreet. A true force to be reckoned with. The only difference is they move in silence, never caring for the spotlight and credit.

I remember one time I was at the gym like any other normal day. (I love working out, and I have always been in decent shape. I'm able to lift a good amount on the bench press, and every man knows that benching gets competitive quickly.)

As I approached the bench press, so did a larger male with the typical cut-off sleeves and a gallon of water — a real gym bro. I started lifting two 45-pound plates on each side. The other guy put on a little more weight than me. After I finished, I decided to go up in weight. This was purely for my own personal growth. I wanted to keep up my fitness goals and continue to progress. I upped the weight, not paying much attention to the guy next to me. I looked over, and this seemed to bother him, so he started to put on more weight than me. This was when I knew that I had encountered an alpha.

I literally was at the gym for my psychical fitness and not for a weightlifting completion. It was too late, though. I had gotten his testosterone going. As I upped more weight, he did it again. Because I was confident in myself, I knew my limitations and capped off, but he was in competition mode. Wanting to show me who was the tougher male, he decided to increase weight one more time. This was where he made a mistake that would hurt him in the end.

This competition in his head clouded his judgment so much that when he went for his second rep, he could not lift it. The bar crushed his chest, and he had to yell for the surrounding guys to lift it off. I remember his face as he was beaten down, huffing and puffing. He was defeated. He was out of breath, and looking down; this man was evidently embarrassed.

Alpha's egos are through the roof. Ego can get you killed or trick you into making horrible decisions. It's made some of the strongest leaders underestimate their opponents and fall. Next time you go to a bar, simply pay attention to the loud males. They're usually either around females trying to impress them or telling war stories, putting down the weaker man encircling them.

All they care about is power and having control over the room and others. Every moment is about asserting their dominance. It drives their every

Lone Wolf Theory

action and move. Alphas thrive off constant competition, power, and control. Alphas are, without a doubt, some of the biggest leaders throughout history, but most of the time, they get consumed by their ego and reputation. It determines their entire identity, so if they lose or get defeated, they shut down.

Alphas and Betas always go with the crowd and never dare to go against what society accepts or deems as normal. It is as if they would literally jump off a bridge if it was deemed cool. Though they are dominant, they crave validation and acceptance. The pack is everything to them. Sigmas, however, are the lone wolves, and they choose to do their own thing no matter what the situation is. It doesn't matter if it's cool or lame. If it doesn't feel right to them, they just don't care. Sigmas do what feels right and what pleases them but never in a selfish way. Psychologists believe this comes mainly from being let down as a kid by friends and family. It's easier not to establish any close ties to an individual for sigmas. It is very rare for them to do so but when they do, best believe they'll love you and have your back until the end.

This mentality makes you see close ties as having anchors attached to them, pulling down the heart. Love holds them down from being free, or they have been through so much pain from getting close to others that they rather avoid close relationships as much as possible. They will cut you off in a split second before you have the chance to get close enough to let them down.

As I have stated earlier, having support and love from the people who are close to us is crucial to getting us through difficult situations. Life throws all

Lone Wolf Theory

sorts of shit at us on a daily basis. Don't get it mixed up, though. Sigmas are some of the strongest leaders and figures in our world. On top of that, they are the innovators who are not scared to think outside of the box from what we consider normal.

Going against the grain and choosing to be a lone wolf has led to some of the greatest medical and scientific discoveries ever. People laughed at the wright brothers for saying they could fly. People got killed for saying the world was round and orbiting the sun. No matter what the example is, every major discovery or breakthrough is only possible by thinking outside of the box. This means looking at things differently from what is considered normal or known. Every single pioneer and innovator was ridiculed for leaving the pack's ideology to think differently.

Alpha vs. Sigma, Choosing to be Alone

Sigmas often get confused with alpha males because they are just as polarizing and charismatic. Even though the sigma does not want control or power, they obtain it with almost no effort. Sigmas have this ability where they can grab the attention from the alpha without even saying a word. They steal the spotlight, and people become mesmerized as though they are attracted to their aura like a magnet. They're that "mysterious guy" that gets all the eyes on him the second he walks into the room. People seem to want to know, "who is that?" Controlling the room while seeming to always be themselves regardless of who's watching them, and they are so relaxed but confident that it seems to just radiate off into the world.

A sigma might not say much when you first meet them, but you can tell they are far from why. What

Lone Wolf Theory

you don't understand is a sigma is 10 steps ahead, always thinking, planning, and surviving. What you don't know is that their low-key persona is a mask they put on so they can read the whole room and determine who would be a waste of their time and who is in investment. This is determined based on how one speaks and caries themselves.

When they do speak, it's not much but also not too little. It seems to come off as vague but very direct. They can relate to everyone, and they listen to everyone without striving for attention. They want to be invisible because, in their experience, companionship slows them down. But somehow, someway, they capture the ears and eyes of the whole crowd, sometimes with the simplest action.

Pay attention next time you're at an event, party, or gathering. They're always there sitting to the side, minding their own business, but yet they grasp your attention with nothing but eye contact leaving you curious. Leading without exerting authority and leaving everyone wondering who that guy is.

I described this personality in detail because a majority of us who struggle with loneliness is like this. Most likely, if you can relate, then you are a lone wolf like me.

Being alone turns us into Sigmas. Embrace it. You can find strength in it. Choosing to act on things alone isn't always a bad thing! It can come with a lot of positives. When you act alone, you know what to expect from yourself for the most part. You know your intentions, motives, and heart's desire, plus it's impossible to deceive yourself or let yourself down. As much as you put trust in others, they can be unreliable and fall short.

People change, and people are selfish; it's human

nature. You just have to be careful and catch yourself when you start feeling alone and depressed. Having your guard up after being broken makes sense to a lot of us. However, it doesn't mean you should block everyone out of your life. Create healthy boundaries, not walls. There must be a balance. You can still find beauty and love in the right people as long as you take the time to feel them out.

If you are a sigma, please find at least one person you trust in your lifetime and treat them right. If they leave or it fails, practice self-love and practice coping skills when the dark thoughts come into your awareness. There is no avoiding these negative thoughts as they will come. I really wish this wasn't how it is, but we are human. Fears and thoughts cripple us. The trick to overcoming it is to find ways to let them pass. They will especially come to infect your brain when you are a lone wolf.

Alpha vs. Sigma, Choosing to be Alone

Knowing this information makes it easier to understand why people develop sigma personality traits. But is it healthy to cut people off and take life head-on by ourselves? What about those who don't choose to leave the pack but instead they're abandoned by the pack?

CHAPTER FOUR
Time Alone

"I'm fascinated with myself and love hearing the sound of my own voice. I'd like to hear what I have to say. A lot of people don't like being alone because they truly don't like themselves, but I love me."

– Gene Simmons

Lone wolves, in some cases, spend their whole adult life living and surviving on their own without ever seeing another wolf. Destined to die alone, roaming for miles in some of the harshest and remote territories in the world. They

Time Alone

are equipped with nothing but their will to survive. The lone wolf is remarkable, but what about humans? What happens when we spend a large amount of our time in complete isolation? Can someone be successful at survival and mental happiness living completely alone as a human?

Let us look at one of the most isolated men known to the world, who claim their mind, body, and spirit have reached a level of understanding of peace and happiness from being alone in their own thoughts. Mauro Morandi abandoned life as he knew it on Italy's Budelli island.

Mauro lived in complete isolation for 32years with small pleasures such as his dog, radio, and coffee. He had no care or stress in the world. This is amazing to me because most teenagers and young adults can't even survive one hour without their cellphone. Yet this man was able to live in complete and utter isolation and not get depressed, bored, or anxious. He was at peace with the absolute bare essentials and silence. Nothing but his thoughts.

This is alien to us in this day and age because we look at this as abnormal. Who is crazy enough to leave friends, family, and the civilized world? Who would leave such comfort and luxury? This is unheard of in the advanced, technological, and super world we have been creating. Life has become so convenient due to technology, but we get lost without our GPS because our parents couldn't read a map up and down.

Mauro had no one to talk to. He was in complete silence and had no interactions, and he claims he was the happiest he has ever been in his life. How is this even possible? Family interactions are proven to be

Time Alone

healthy and reduce stress and anxiety, but what happens when you do not have that, or you push it away? It has shown that being alone takes a great mental and emotional strain on our minds and bodies. We are social creatures, and there is no way around that. Most of us feel depressed or wasted away if we stay home and do nothing all day. Some people do it by choice even.

If this man on an island found happiness and peace when being alone, then how is it that there are so many people who claim that being alone is the worst feeling they have ever felt in life?

Unlike the man who lived alone, most of us don't have the mindset to not crave attention, love, and social interaction. Being acknowledged by others is almost like a drug to some people. Being on your own seems to have the complete opposite effect on your average everyday person. Lack of connection with people will and can make you depressed, suicidal, violent, and even insane. It creates a disconnection between happiness and a healthy mindset. Once again were forced to look at the duality of being alone.

A large number of teens and young adults claim to be or feel the loneliest. Their brains are not fully developed when they start getting flooded with hormones. This leads to they easily being a chemical imbalance that leads to severe mood swings. It is an undeniable fact that they are the most depressed and the most likely to commit suicide, more than any other age range. On top of that, having no strong family or friends intensifies these tragedies and mental health conditions. The odds are stacked against them in their adolescent mind.

If that wasn't enough stress, some of these kids

Time Alone

go through so much pain and hardships in their personal life just to get bullied and unnoticed in school. Imagine getting fucked with in school and left out just to come home to an unstable environment after that with no support? I understand and sympathize with the youth. It is such a fragile time when you start to grow and form the habits that you will carry into your adulthood. Once again, these situations will make or break you, but other people will get pushed to mental insanity and commit horrible crimes like shooting up a school, cutting themselves, or abusing hard drugs to numb the pain. Others want to break the cycle, and others take the positive route and focus on school or sports to escape their conditions. We have to watch out for the youth, especially the ones at risk with broken homes and no social gratification.

They are the most fragile, and a simple

compliment or hello could stop them from doing something unspeakable. But in all seriousness, how can some people in these circumstances be able to find happiness and the ability to want to wake up and survive every day?

Even as a kid, I couldn't sit alone with my thoughts for more than one minute. I needed constant distractions or attention. As I got older, I even put on the bad boy imagine. It felt good to have eyes on me and to be respected. At the time, I would not admit that it was to stick out for attention.

As I aged, I started to notice that no matter how tough or cool I would appear to others, it would never truly fill the emptiness I had. I craved the love you feel from family, friends, and a close partner. Every time I got a taste of it, I felt euphoria, and when that love left me, I felt rage. Every time I was

Time Alone

left with my thoughts in the end. I wanted to watch the world burn.

One time the lights went out, and I was alone in my bed. This is the time that everyone is truly in their head. Before you go to sleep, your deepest thoughts, concerns and fears run through your brain. These are thoughts that you don't share with others. There was no true way to mask or distract yourself from what concerns you and bothers you. Your fears and regrets are amplified. True loneliness would start to set in, and I had no one I could trust or share my thoughts with.

It is easy for me to explain the lone wolf theory because I am speaking from experience. I have been in some of the darkest places in my life alone, with my brain working against me. No phone to distract myself, no video games, and no car to drive away with. There was no one to open up to or share my life with; I was a mess in my head. I just needed to vent these ideas, but criticisms of myself would come up, and I had no way to push them out, burry them, or forget so I could move on.

This made it so easy to go slip into negative thought patterns. It wasn't until I was older that I truly was able to sit in silence and reflect without catastrophizing my life in the current moment. My mother had bought me a book that I never cared to read. I just skimmed through it, but when she passed, I decided to read it more in-depth. It was ***Shamballa: The Sacred Path of the Warrior*** by Chogyam Trungpa. We could get deep into the lessons from this book, but for time's sake, this book taught me how to turn my rage and violent outbursts into positivity to accomplish things.

Time Alone

There were two times I had to be utterly alone with nothing but myself, alone with no cell phone, no distractions, no friends, no family, and no lover. That was when I was in jail. My mother was sick of my shit and kicked me out of the house. We will get into details about my struggles later.

After falling on my ass so much, I was eventually forced to look at myself and my behaviors and what led me to such shitty outcomes in my life. It wasn't until I was about 25 that I finally figured out how to handle my thoughts. I was the architect of my own destruction, and my dumb ass was blaming it on not having a strong support system.

I used to get so angry and depressed, and I dealt with it very negatively, making very impulsive decisions because of how I felt. In the long run, I let my toxic thoughts dictate my actions, but it did nothing but hurt me. I would fight, curse people out, walk out on good opportunities, and more. I pushed everyone away until I had no one to lean on.

Looking back, it makes me sick how destructive I was. When my bright ideas came, I didn't run them by anyone or stop to think; I would just react. Changing was not an overnight journey. After bumping my head for years, I finally was able to not ignore my conscious or common sense.

Slowly but surely, I would at least acknowledge them and, at the same time, not react or dwell on them when they were unhealthy thoughts. For once in my life, I could play out the tape before I decided to punch someone in the face. I began to see the difference between wrong and right, even when I didn't agree.

So how do we turn around sitting in our own thoughts? Especially when they begin to become

Time Alone

crippling to our mental health and growth. The easy answer would be going to talk to someone or see your support group. But we are lone wolves, and our options tend to be limited. Some of us simply do not have the support system needed to pull through.

What worked for me was being able to play out the tape of what would happen if I acted on these thoughts. If I hurt someone physically, mentally, or verbally, all it will do is dig my hole deeper and push me farther from having friends, family, or a partner. Being destructive makes others not want to be around us. When you act selfishly, others see you as a Cancer. No one wants to get cancer.

The last way I delt with my issues with no support was to come up with tools and activities that allowed time to go by so that I could calm down, such as exercise, writing, Art, and other outlets that you enjoy. Find a way to release your frustrations without destroying your life in the process. Creation is expression. Expression is therapy.

I promise I have been there. I have made horrible decisions with some of the worst consequences that I had to face. No matter how justified I felt, I knew I was wrong deep in my heart. I would do something wild, and in the morning, I always felt stupid for my actions. I remember wishing I had calmed down and thought at the moment before overreacting.

Some conflicts and circumstances are really not worth the freak outs. Just breathe. Feelings may hurt in the morning, but eventually, they will pass. You'll be able to think rationally again if you just give yourself sometime before making a bad decision.

No one wants to look like a victim because it's embarrassing, and no one wants to be a bitch. I get it. But one day after the smoke settles, your maturity will bring clarity. Sometimes it is not worth beating the bricks out of someone and going to jail, when you could have just lifted some weights or hit a punching bag.

A lot of people take their love and support for granted. They don't know what it's like to lose that. Some people have no choice but to sit in their thoughts, alone with no form of coping skills. Solitary confinement has been proven to be ineffective and inhumane.

Thousands of government officials and outreach workers are working tirelessly to end this form of punishment used on violent inmates who will not listen. What we have been learning is that taking away small interactions from the criminally insane and violent does more long-term damage in the end.

Of course, it's evident that some of these

criminals will never be able to function in society or be able to put their violet tendencies aside. It just shows that having simple human interaction and support makes a huge impact on our mood and mental state.

In 2018, a prison decided to give death row inmates pet cats to take care of in their cells. Now I don't agree with or cosign with what these prisoners did but what happened goes to show what simple interactions can do. After a few months, the prisoners started to show less aggression and more compassion. They were treating the guards with respect and pampering their cats. They even started to show more responsibility by cleaning their cells and caring for the animal. Some burst into tears and had emotional breakdowns. It's as if they put their criminal attitude away in the mean time. Interacting

Time Alone

with a cat softened the heart of violent psychopathic prisoners. Their isolation made them more aggressive, but simply adding a cat calmed them down.

There are even some people in this world who choose silence by choice. People travel to temples and churches to seek a spiritual state of being through silence. This is known as a vow of silence. It is said that shutting out conversation with other humans for long periods of time heightens senses, raises spirituality, channels your innermost thoughts, and connects you to the earth and your purpose.

How can someone with almost the same circumstances as a lack of human interaction have such different results? On top of that, they're choosing to disconnect! No one is born a monk. A lot of these men leave their lives behind and choose this lifestyle. They have cars, homes, families, and identities. They give it all away to sit in silence.

Catholic/Christian monks and Buddhist monks sit in silence for long periods of time, even for years. These are two completely different religions, yet they both claim it leads to an inner calm and that those simple sounds we take for granted, like the rustle of leaves or gusts of wind, take on a new quality.

CHAPTER FIVE
Fighting Your Own Battles

"Another of the hard things about being in a war, grandchildren, is that although there are times of quiet when the fighting has stopped, you know you will soon be fighting again. Those quiet times give you the chance to think about what has happened. Some of it you would rather not think about as you remember the pain and the sorrow. You also have time to worry about what will happen when you go into battle again."

– Joseph Bruchac, **Code Talker: A Novel About the Navajo Marines of World War Two**

Fighting Your Own Battles

Choosing to be on your own or being forced to be on your own is never an easy thing. Everyone on this earth wants to be loved and this is no secret. Now we know that we can be pushed to the point of extreme isolation and we cannot deny it.

It seems to stem from severe neglect, trauma, and let down. Surviving this life of solitude comes with blood, sweat, tears, and a lot of long cold lonely nights. You find yourself with your back against the wall with no one to lean on. Being alone means you have to be resourceful, quick, and calculated. There is absolutely no room for error. Once you fuck up, you're finished, plus this life we live is always coming to knock you on your ass.

People will not understand your struggle. You have been built tough because you have no one to bail you out, no backup, and no reinforcements. You are a killer and survivor without a pack to back you up. Remember the normal that wolves hunt in packs, so when they cannot take on a hunt or battle, they have their peers to help them survive. But you're a lone wolf. You're on your own, and it will be fucking difficult.

Wolves are apex predators that eat, hunt, and fight till their last breath to survive. We like to believe that because we are humans, we are more civilized, but in reality, we have to hunt, fight and survive in the human reality we have created. You're going to get hungry, so what are you going to do when you start to feel the hunger and pain? What are you going to do when you're attacked? You have to come up with ways to eat, survive and fight back or you will, without a doubt, die. Same thing goes for the human culture we have established. Feeling hunger and physical pain will make you into an animal. Your instincts will take over your whole way of being. For you, this is not a game; it's life or death.

I say life and death only because you have more to lose than the woman or man next to you. Having this feeling from physical and mental strife is nothing but pure jet fuel to succeed. Start to look at it as your biggest advantage and not a crippling weakness. It gives you an edge over everyone else who didn't experience this. Struggle gives you thick skin over your feelings and armor over your heart; you're ready for battle.

Being prepared makes you more resilient in life. Once again, this is one thing for sure that is promised in this world. That promise is that when it rains, it fucking pours. Fortunately, your misfortunes

Lone Wolf Theory

made you tough as nails. You're rough around the edges, but hey, you know what to do when shit hits the fan.

Having no back up is a reality for people like us so. Keep this in your mind when you're pushing through life. Life is a never-ending drama sinking in the sand below your feet. What are you going to do when your back's up against the wall? Fight or give up? Giving up is the fastest and easiest way out. It's an ejection out of your cockpit that brings you back to your safety, comfort, and misery. Many grow old and tell stories of how they regret wasting time and not taking a risk. We all have potential, but we trick ourselves into burying it and hiding it from the world. Accepting your circumstances is defeat.

This mentality of giving in to your circumstances will end you and your life, and it will be over sooner than later. But here is the thing you need to understand. You're potentially cheating yourself out of living the same life as some of the most successful and happy people in the world. You just gave up without even an ounce of fight in you. You could have been an astronaut, a president, or just a good fucking guy with a family, a wife, and a medium-sized house. But you didn't want to fight through and survive, grow and expand. Instead, you threw up the white flag and let yourself go. Pushing on was too tough, and giving up was the easier thing to do.

Fighting a war is never easy, and I never said it was. Moving through life is war, without a doubt. We will have to fight this war till our bitter end. Being alive feels like a long war that we can never win, but in reality, war is only won through battles. What we forget is that every day is a battle we have to fight.

Lone Wolf Theory

These battles are presented to us in all sorts of situations. There are intense battles, such as getting cancer, getting fired, or your car breaking down. There are more positive battles, like overcoming your fears, going on a job interview, and getting stage freight. These battles are daily and will not end until our life is over. You cannot get out of this war. We have to fight unless we become defeated and let it go. Choosing not to fight in these battles results in defeat.

We can become depressed, suicidal addicts, criminals, and even homeless if we do not fight. So why not fight then? You have a chance to win. Even if you lose, you know you tried. Understand that you will never face full defeat if you get up and fight.

Underdogs have won through things like history, sports, and life. Nothing is guaranteed, and all that

Fighting Your Own Battles

matters is who fights the hardest to win, even in adversity. Fighting these battles on your own can be terrifying when you have no team to help you out in the field. Ultimately, if you lose, it's game over.

I like comparing between boxing and football. If you get knocked out in boxing, you get knocked the fuck out, and everyone sees it and knows you were the one that got knocked out. When you lose a game in football, everyone sees you, but instead, it's the whole team that blew it. Having no team puts a lot of pressure on you to win. And when you don't, you will get knocked out with no one else to lose with you. Lone wolves have no teammates to help them win when boxing in the ring.

This is one cold-ass world. We all wish we could be with petter pan and never grow up. Being an adult sucks for a large majority of people. We have to work and hustle to eat so we can pay bills and obtain things to live a stable, secure life. Working, getting money, paying bills, and getting groceries is our version of hunting to survive.

Human necessities are what make us safe, comfortable, and alive. We need a place to eat, shower, and sleep to have a fighting chance in this world. Learning how to hunt and eat on your own takes great skill. Like anything else that is learned, some obtain greater skill than others. The skill of your hunt reflects your haul. Hunters on top are the ones who get bigger kills, and the ones with less skill get nothing. We call it the rich, the poor, and the middle class.

Regardless of your skill, we are dead if we don't go out there and obtain resources for our home. There's a cliché saying that you've probably heard from an older person. It goes like this, "catch a man a fish and he will eat for a day, teach him how to fish, and you feed him for a lifetime." We realized we were on our own, and it sucks. Stop making excuses, and learn how to live by your intuition. Teaching yourself how to fight and survive will set you up with life skills that will give you an edge over others. Things like school, life skills, and hustles will keep us fed for our whole lives. Look at gaining more knowledge and skills as an asset to making your life more bountiful and fuller of fruits. Sulking won't move the needle for us. We can't use our loneliness to destroy the last of what we have. We have to turn our weaknesses into strengths. Don't you get it?

Turning the negatives of being alone into positives will motivate you. Once you find that motivation, it's like jet fuel in your brain, and you fight your battles head-on, and then one day, the fighting won't be so hard. This is because you'll have enough battle scars that you'll know what to do in the war that we fight called life.

When I first moved out of my mother's home, simple life responsibilities hit me hard. This was the first time that I had to do things on my own, and it was a rude awakening. If I did not get groceries or clean my place, no one would do it for me. I had to go out there and "hunt" every single day, or I wouldn't make it.

Whether we decided to leave our pack or our pack left us, the simple fact is that if we do not wake up and "hunt," we will starve. If we starve, then we die. This is what sets us apart from the regulars. We are in a battle for survival, and we are fighting uphill battles on our own. Fighting our own battles takes a toll on our minds and souls. There are dents in the armor we wear around our hearts and scars in the

Fighting Your Own Battles

thick skin that covers us.

Figuring out how to have situational awareness and how to act right will save our ass in the long run. I'll give you an example. If you have a coworker who keeps taunting you and provoking you, and you have tried everything from ignoring them to walking away, one day, when he crosses the line and catches you on a bad day, you just snap and punch him in the face. Now you have lost your job, you're in jail, and will be behind bills. You lost the battle. That guy probably has a family, a wife, and friends to support him. You have to stop and think you have more to lose. This does not make you weak for walking away or ignoring them. We are stronger than these types of people. When real-life shit happens, we have to know how to react. We don't just break down and cry, remember that.

Lone Wolf Theory

Having to go out there and get it on your own creates satisfaction unlike no other. I don't think I'd enjoy the small things in life and be grateful if I didn't have to bust my ass on my own to get to where I wanted to be. Nothing was handed to me. I'm a lone fucking wolf. I came up on my own, and I'm fierce.

People psych themselves out and think it's impossible to accomplish and change on their own or be on their own. I promise that once you get a taste of change and success, it is an out-of-body experience. It will motivate you to go out into this world and conquer it. One day you will realize that your fears are nothing. Normal people will never understand the tears you shed and the dark pit you hold in your soul, and that is ok. Everyone is constantly fighting their own battles to be free from their past. We are not less than; we just have to do it alone. It's the only way to create a sustainable and happy future for yourself. The battles will get easier, but the war will never end.

CHAPTER SIX
Making the Best of What You Have

"Did you hear about the rose that grew from a crack in the concrete? Proving nature's law is wrong, it learned to walk without having feet. Funny it seems, but by keeping its dreams, it learned to breathe fresh air. Long live the rose that grew from /2concrete when no one else ever cared."

– Tupac Shakur

I have only ever been spiritual and never religious, but I truly believe God put us here and made us all different. I started to believe life is too complex

Making the Best of What You Have

and beautiful for there to be a god. Some of it sucks, but it's as if the dark side is a test that breaks us or makes us. Being abandoned is not for the weak-hearted. It evolves us and can potentially make some of us stronger and more resilient. Sadly it can do the opposite as well. The weak-hearted seem to die off from the intensity of the emotions attached to it.

Whether being abandoned by my close friends or mother or choosing to be alone after being betrayed, I always seemed to make my life worse. Being alone enraged me and with anger came terrible life choices made off out of emotional impulses. I was a ticking time bomb, ready to self-destruct.

It came in all forms, whether it was going to jail, losing my girl, getting into fights, etc. I could go on forever with all the reckless shit I did in my younger years. Whatever it was, I never took accountability for what I was doing, and it made my situation worse. It was everyone's fault, and they were disloyal for leaving me behind. I never admitted that I was acting like a piece of shit because I couldn't cope with loss or being alone. I was always acting like the victim because I got left behind in every aspect of love.

I gave up on fighting to get out of this hole and slipped into a darker depression, making my hole deeper day in and day out. I was stuck. I had isolated myself to the point that I was pretty much alone. Completely and utterly on my own. People had already left me, and anyone new I met saw that I didn't give a fuck, so they created distance.

No one wants to be around that. Everything was on me at this point. Just like it does on anyone else, I got into a lot of sticky situations, and I didn't know how I got through on my own. I pushed myself to a

Making the Best of What You Have

breaking point where my mind, heart, and soul felt a need to change. True and pure struggle will motivate some people.

I have a friend who lost everything and had to humble himself to take a bus. He was embarrassed and ashamed. He had a mustang the year before and crashed it drunk driving and got arrested. After that, he lost their job to make matters worse, and he stopped paying insurance at the time to try to save the money so he couldn't replace his car. He refused to give up and accept his situation, so he kept taking the bus and saving. Finally, he got a piece of shit Honda and kept going to work. Eventually, he got a raise and promotion after a year. He drives a matte black Corvette now.

He could have easily said fuck this and quit. One thing I do know is that feeling the struggle and consequences of my actions triggered a change in my life and behavior. It was a spark that lit a fire under my ass. After falling on my face so much, I was eventually forced to look at myself and notice the actions that led me to shitty outcomes in my life.

Most of the time, it was me who would make a situation bad or even worse. I didn't understand that anger and depression were something I would have to overcome. These emotions were shackles on my hands, feet, and mind. Rebelling and fighting life just put a tighter chokehold around you.

We all have common sense, right? Well, when a hole is deeper, it's harder to get out of. Why make life harder when you are already starting behind the ball? You are at a disadvantage, and you already have to bust your ass harder. You're not the person whose mom does their laundry and still cuts their fruit up.

Making the Best of What You Have

Embrace it; don't internalize it.

I remember I used to get so angry and envious seeing kids who were spoiled with love and gifts from their families. Being forced to be independent and choosing to isolate made me strong, but I could not shake the jealousy of close-knit families and couples I had seen in public. I would always get a sick feeling in the pit of my stomach. No matter what I did, I could not shake the jealousy and hate I had for people who had love.

I even remember hating the holiday season. It put a heavy toll on my soul. Thanksgiving and Christmas always made me want to throw out every turkey and burn every Christmas tree. During the holidays, when I had to go to the store to get groceries and things for my place, I would get so upset. Seeing people getting ready for their big family festivities reminded me of my depression and struggles. I would cringe at their happiness and joy because I knew I was going to be all by myself. It was so easy to say poor me or that I'm not good enough.

This mindset is poison, and it made me bitter for years. Nothing changed until I realized that the time I would waste sitting around sulking, I could be out there hunting and surviving so I could change and make it out. I could be making my life better one hunt at a time, with or without anyone. The responsibility for the outcome of your life lies solely on your actions and decisions. People will give you sympathy, but at the end of the day, humans are selfish, and they're not in your body. They really don't care, and it's not their responsibility to care or to even give you a helping hand. You have to make changes on your own because no one will do it for

Making the Best of What You Have

you. If you don't, you will be stuck in the same place with the same circumstances until you attempt to do something about it to change it.

You honestly cannot be mad at people for being born into the family God chose for them. It was part of their destiny and life lessons. Who, what, when, and how will forever be beyond any of our control. You will go insane trying to solve something that none of us will ever understand. Remember not to get hung up on someone's perfect appearance. Believe me. All that glitters isn't gold. These perfect people and brady bunch families have their problems behind closed doors. Some of those model families have some of the nastiest fights and arguments, but they just hide it to uphold an image. Even some of those rich families are in so much debt and on credit from their lifestyle, attempting to show off to others. At the end of the day, just worry about yourself and make your situation better for yourself.

Sooner or later, a new pack will find you when you are not even looking. They will be drawn to you without even being aware. Humans pick up auras without even knowing it. Have you ever not wanted to get personal with someone because something just doesn't feel right? This is because you are picking up on their negative energy.

A person's aura is the energy that comes from within them. Your aura is the vibe that your body naturally gives off in the world. We are made of energy. Energy is the life of the universe. People subconsciously feel auras, others are able to pick them up, but most are totally unaware. Our energy is a magnet, and it brings like-minded people towards other like-minded people. Once you stop forcing love and success, it seems to just come to you. When you attract and don't seek it, it just happens, and it seems to be one of the proven laws of the universe.

Making the Best of What You Have

No one is entitled to love you, so here is a rude awakening for you. The world keeps on spinning and time keeps ticking, and it is cruel. This world waits on no one. Knowing this, why wouldn't you put in your all every single day? I mean, what is the worst that could happen if you fight to live or you do nothing and let yourself die out? I personally would rather die knowing I tried to change than die old and decrepit giving up angry and upset.

I know it sucks to end up in a state of complete and utter self. You're all by yourself through life on holidays, special days, and bad days, and every day it's just you. You feel cheated out of having friends, family, and lovers, as these people are supposed to catch us when we fall and show us what they learned along the way. But guess what? You have to grow up and get over it. This is your reality, and not a single tear will make it better. Let it out, wipe them away, and buckle down because it is time to fix your fucking life. You only have one! No one's going to fix it for you. Stop wasting your whole life blaming others for the past. You're in the shit now, not them.

Don't sit in your shit and let it ferment. All self-blame does is slowly kill you and make your life stink more than it did the day before. Please carry on. We can't give up now. We have to get up, get to it and keep moving. You have to make the best of what you have, period. We have one life, and that is it. God dealt some of us a shitty hand, but the only way to get to the jackpot depends on how we play the hand we were given.

Always be humble and grateful even when it's a struggle to do so. I know you don't want to hear that same line that adults use to guilt trip you with, but it's true, so I'm saying it. Things could always be worse, but hey, it's fucking true. There are kids out here with cancer, people who lost their legs, and

Making the Best of What You Have

they're out there fighting hard. Fighting to survive and fighting for happiness. If they got the balls to wake up every day and keep moving, then what is your excuse? Sorry I'm so assertive, but I just want to get the point across. Your feelings are valid feeling what you felt was key to me implementing a new lifestyle.

Don't ever think that it is weak when you feel down about being on your own. Your soul and heart are trying to speak to you. We are just human. It's in our inner being to be loved and supported by those around us. Do not be ashamed. Being alone makes us stronger when shit happens, and we just know what to do when other people freak out. High-stress situations are our specialty. We're cool, calm, and collected.

There will always be bumps in the road that slow

us down. No one is immune. These things happen when you're the president of the United States or some crazy cat lady. It's fucking life. Love yourself through the thunderstorm, and eventually, it will stop raining, and the sun will come out. Love is all we need. Just learn to get it from within, and outside, love will come to us like a magnet.

I say this because love, unfortunately, comes and goes. It can make us so warm and fuzzy, but in the blink of an eye, it can burn us to the core. Love... we can't live with it, and we can't live without it. It's something that helps us to keep trudging through this tough, cold world. We have to accept love when it leaves as much as we accept love when it comes. We need to love ourselves to make it through the cold nights alone. And trust me, you'll have them.

Even if you are fortunate to find your best friend or your life partner, they are humans. They will have

Making the Best of What You Have

off days and busy days. You need to practice self-love; it is the only love that burns eternally. It burns till the end of your time; it is the love you have for yourself.

You know yourself the best, so you know how to love yourself the best. Treat yourself by reaffirming yourself. Calm yourself down and treat yourself self even if it's a simple haircut or doing your nails. Learn to do what you love. The key to surviving alone is learning to love yourself, as I can't stress it enough. Once you do this, it will radiate off you, and before you know it, you'll attract a new pack, and with a new pack will come new love.

Loving yourself will always be your fallback when you're truly alone, and all love is lost. It will mend you up and heal you up over time. It will radiate off you, and the law of attraction will turn you into a beacon that attracts love right to you with ease. Once you find love for yourself, you'll start making better choices.

We have to live by choice not chance. If we take a chance, we leave it up to others and the world to dictate our outcome. It's easier for us to give up than to just take our life by the reigns and start steering it in a better direction. You don't build the Great Wall of China overnight. It takes one brick, then another brick, all placed in the right order. If you make a choice to make one good decision after another, slowly but surely, your life will improve, I promise you.

Start small with daily goals to reach the bigger picture, and that mountain won't be so intimidating anymore. Accomplishments and self-improvements take longer to see results, but I got a bigger high from any drug or sex I had in my entire life. All these quick

Making the Best of What You Have

rushes give a rush of good feeling, but it's just a band-aid. Once it wears off, you're stuck with yourself again and that feel good didn't do shit. You're back where you started and forced to deal with the same problems that you didn't decide to work on and change.

I knew this girl who couldn't stop drinking. She was so beautiful, but inside, she was damaged. Sex, alcohol, and partying made her forget her past and insecurities. Every time she woke up, she would feel like shit throwing up, and feeling miserable, and you could see the depression on her face. She wasn't the same person she was last night when she was drunk. I'm not saying you can't have some drinks; it's just an example of how easily we can get lost in distractions because we want to heal our loneliness.

None of us signed up for life, but we have to deal

Lone Wolf Theory

with it now, and no one has all the answers. I've been there feeling how you feel hopeless, depressed, and ready to end it to not feel so lonely. Just because we are abandoned by our pack or we leave doesn't mean we can't work on ourselves and change to find a new pack that will take us in. I wrote this book for the loners. Embrace your situation no matter how painful it is. Get the tears out, and don't dwell on it. Crying about it won't change it. The only thing that will change is we wanting to change and putting in the work. If nothing changes, then nothing changes. I know we don't know each other, but I can relate to how you feel having to do this on your own. Keep fighting to survive and don't quit before the miracle comes. I love you.

CHAPTER SEVEN
Being Ok With Being Alone

"If there's a single lesson that life teaches us, it's that wishing doesn't make it so. Words and thoughts don't change anything. Language and reality are kept strictly apart — reality is tough, unyielding stuff, and it doesn't care what you think or feel or say about it. Or it shouldn't. You deal with it, and you get on with your life."

– Lev Grossman, The Magicians

Learning to live your life on your own is the key to your success and your mental sanity. I am talking about being able to live it to its fullest potential too. I want you to get better, and I want you to repair and rebuild your sense of family and love one day, but nothing is ever perfect. You must understand that even if you find your tribe that there will be days that you will have to be there for yourself.

The world does not always revolve around you. People get busy or just simply can't always be on your side due to obligations or circumstances. This requires the ability to reach the mental level of being ok. You need to be able to sit with yourself and your own thoughts. In other words, it is critical to reach a point where you are comfortable in your own skin without needing someone to make you feel complete. Being able to train yourself to live with the fear of being alone is like treating and removing a tumor before it spreads. It can go into remission but always lingers within us with the ability to come back and bring us to our knees again. Loneliness can make us do dumb shit again, whether it's drugs, sex, impulsive spending, or gambling, etc. Being alone makes us do dumb shit so we can feel ok or temporarily happy. The side effects of loneliness can be just like cancer. It will kill you if not treated properly and correctly.

I remember I was so lost from going through life on my own, but I am grateful because it really forced me to find myself. I finally came to the conclusion that accepting your situation will liberate your mind indefinitely.

Acceptance will take the invisible shackles off your mental and spiritual prison. From there, you will begin to realize your true identity. In return, this will truly make you feel free, happy, and content with your life in its current state. Reaching that true inner peace with self happens only when you finally feel that it's ok to be alone. This lesson is so simple, yet it had the power to turn me into a man. Now looking back in hindsight, I can see that in order for me to become wise, I had to start out as a fool.

I remember my loneliness was so bad at one point that I couldn't even leave my house. I knew I didn't want to be alone, but I convinced myself that no one wanted to be around me. I told myself I was ugly, undesirable, a troublemaker, and the last option for everyone and anyone. I literally poised my mind with my own negative beliefs instead of taking the positives out of my experiences. How was I supposed to find and attract love if I won't even leave my own house because I cared about what people will think about me?

You will never attract a new tribe if isolating

yourself in your home is your vibe. Once you understand that you will not get along with everyone or that not everyone will be attracted to you, then you can tolerate rejection. Suck it up and put yourself out there. Eventually 1 out of 10 people you go out and build will be a solid brick in the life you're rebuilding. I eventually got out and built amazing relationships by giving myself a chance to meet those amazing people. Knowing that I could finally be comfortable in my own skin, I eventually nursed myself through these lonely times. I discovered that I could be alone even though most people cannot be alone. I didn't need to talk to anyone, and I could talk to myself. Through my isolation, I found my highest mental elevation. My greatest epiphanies came from sitting in silence and going deep within my mind. I felt like Buddha under the bodhi tree finally reaching a higher level of understanding.

This pain is temporary, and just like everything else, it eventually will pass. We will continue to breathe, and babies will bear, and people will die. Let go of the anxieties and get out there. Go on dates. Go out alone to the bar. Pick up hobbies where you will meet people who like what you also are into. I mean how are you going to meet anyone if you just stay in your home all day! That is literally the equivalent of wanting to be in shape but going to the gym and just staring at the weights. You need to put in the work to see the results that you're asking for. Grow a pair and get over rejection. It happens to all of us until we find people who cherish us.

We seem to torture ourselves by doing the same routines and habits day in and day out and wondering why nothing has changed or improved.

Have you ever opened the fridge thinking something new would appear? Nothing comes, and your mom yells at you to close it. Albert Einstein famously said insanity is doing the same thing and expecting different results. So why keep doing the things that made us and kept us lonely? Don't be a dumbass and try new routines and behaviors. It's your life that we're talking about here!

It's hard to get back to the place we once were after being so damaged. We fill the void with pleasure that never seems to fully satisfy our desires. However, I promise you that finding what makes you happy again will put a smile back onto your face. You eventually must heal, accept and let go but finding healthy distractions will buy you time until you're ready to heal. I have found peace in simple hobbies, arts, sports, and other healthy outlets. It honestly really doesn't matter what it is as long as it is something that gets your frustrations out. Challenging yourself will make you smile and distract you from looking at the clock and thinking negative thoughts. To me, that's a good enough reason to get active and productive. It helps pass by some time so you don't feel hopeless.

We all know this world is far from perfect. It is flat-out unfair. It is a cold bitch; I mean, I really don't know why babies die, and serial killers live until they're old. I don't understand any of this, and none of us except God will. All we can control is our actions and our feelings toward the world around us.

Karma is real, and I don't care what religion. They all have the same core of karmic values. These values seem to all hold similar lessons and teachings. One we hear in many stories and teaching sounds like this. If you walk through life being the best, you will be rewarded, and if you act like a piece of shit, the universe will take from you. I know no one's perfect. I have days where I am cranky and rude or snap. It's not about being perfect, but it's about admitting your wrongs, then correcting them and doing your best to be a better person.

One of the best remedies to help live with your loneliness is giving back by helping and teaching those who are a couple of steps behind you. Learn to help others who are alone and show them what you have learned along the way. You will eventually come across someone who reminds you of yourself when you were in that mindset. It will pain you to see them struggling, so take them under your wing and show them the way. Many will fail because they will not take your guidance and advice. However, it will all be worth it in the end when one person gets guided in the right direction because you woke them up. When you pull the right one up, you will be amazed by the miracle as they turn from a caterpillar to a butterfly.

Watching someone obtain their life and happiness back will be one of the most rewarding experiences you will ever have. Once you receive the knowledge, your job is to pull up those who haven't figured it out yet. Take someone out of the trenches. It can even be done simply by just sharing your story. That, in itself, could be the motivation that some people need to tip their scales in the right direction.

Stop thinking about yourself and be the light in someone's darkness. Shit, seeing someone struggling might even help you forget your problems for once. It's like it makes you realize things could be a lot worse and to be grateful. I promise you, helping others will fill an empty heart. There is something about doing something for someone else without selfishness. It is so rewarding that it strikes a chord in the deepest parts of our souls.

Stop being selfish and share what you did to change the outcome of your life. Seeing others where you used to be will remind you of where you don't want to go back to. Time is something that most of us do not value or take into consideration until we start to age. We start to understand that it is not a renewable resource. It can't be bought, and it can't be created. Time is all we seem to really have at the end of the day. You will start to see that there is a lot of time to spare when you have no one to care for or be with.

Learn to utilize your time alone to make

something of yourself and gain momentum in a positive direction. Use it as a time to reflect, regardless of the fact that silence may be what is causing you to be down in the dumps. Take into account that silence means fewer distractions. Sulking, crying, and staying in bed seems to be all that you're capable of doing, but in reality, your clock is ticking, and time is just wasting away. I know it's hard to gather up the motivation, but you could be using the time alone to learn skills, work on projects and develop tangible things that will aid in your success.

Instead of sitting around upset at the world, you could be sitting around figuring out how to run a business, how to do stocks, and how to create a piece of art. The possibilities are endless. Sure, we make excuses like we can't afford college or that we don't have enough funds to start this. They are all fucking excuses. We live in an age where you can google and YouTube anything you want to learn or get a book that will teach you skills for not even a fraction of the price of college.

Take advantage! I mean, what else are you going to do with all of this spare time? Stop fucking around. We can't buy more time so make it count. If you take the advice from this book and apply it eventually, you will get to where you're trying to go. Things won't be rocky forever. Eventually, your life balances out, and you obtain the family, friends, and spouse. From that time, everything may appear to be back in order. That dark lonely part of your life starts to become a distant memory of your past.

I mean, that's the point of this book. I want you to get back to a sense of love with yourself and others. You also need to be prepared to be back in that situation at any given time. Life is unpredictable, and in a flash, you can lose everything because nothing is guaranteed to last. I'm not wishing ill on you or trying to put that energy in the air but be prepared. People die, and people also walk out of your life with no rhyme or reason. You have to be mentally prepared for this in case it happens again, and you're back to square one.

Being prepared and armed with the skills to cope with being alone will ease the pain. It would be ignorant not to gather the tools to fix your life if it decides to break down again. Remember you're only in control of your actions, and you may want someone to do something or ask them to, but if they don't want to, they simply won't. People have free will for a reason, and you can't do shit sometimes, scary, huh?

People want to impress people naturally. Sometimes we do it without thinking about what con-sequences come from our actions. Do not compromise your beliefs or values because you want people in your life. I started to act out of character to attract people because I was tired of being on my own, but it was not a long-term solution. It will work temporarily, but these bonds will be weak because you are not being your genuine self within the connection. I was guilty of this to the T.

I was able to blend in with whatever crowd I was entertaining. It was like being a chameleon. If someone who liked basketball came to me, then I would talk about basketball, and if someone came around me who liked baseball, I would act like I liked baseball. It was fake, but I just felt like I needed company.

When you do this, you will attract the wrong people because you're building a foundation on something that is not truly you. You will be able to keep it up for a little, but your true self will show, and you will have wasted all that time just to be alone again. Quality over quantity is what matters. Also, you cannot buy friendship and love. I don't care who you are.

We always see the super-rich, out-of-shape man with an attractive model in Miami and LA. We all know she is only there for what he has, not because she loves him. Strip away that man's material, and his soul is bare. Even Mike Tyson used to talk about how he would spend hundreds and thousands on his friends and entourage, and everyone loved him. When he finally ran off the rails and lost everything, no one seemed to stick around or even have his back.

At his lowest and darkest, everyone had left him behind to rot.

Be careful of being too generous. You will attract leeches. Humans are naturally greedy. They will put up with you and, in secret, dislike you to obtain personal gain. Once this is accomplished or you run out of resources, their true colors will present themselves. They become manipulative, sticking around just to tell you what you want to hear to please you. They will even do it when they know they're giving you terrible advice.

A real friend or lover will call you out on your bullshit because they don't want you to fuck up or they generally care about you. If you crash out for people like this, they will scatter when it gets real, and once again, it will be the same story of you being alone. Back to square one. Learn who is real and who is fake by not overly giving to people when you first meet them. You will see who cares about you and not about what you have. Lastly you need to learn to cut ties with your past.

I know it is easier said than done, but you need to understand that we are not our past. This means that you possess the power to no longer be victims of it. Holding onto your past mistake is an anchor. It's unnecessary baggage that you need to cut loose. Until we discover time travel, there is absolutely nothing you can do to change it. All you can do is forgive yourself and others and release it for good.

This sense of doubt and less then is all in our heads. You are your own worst critic; snap the fuck out of it. Every day is a new opportunity to undo the damage that has been done. The tears will make your soul beautiful, and the let-downs will make your aura stronger.

Take action in your life even if you look back and you're the only one standing up for yourself. No one else is going to do it for you. There is no easy way to do this or bear it with a broken heart. I just hope that I got your mind thinking from this book. I hope I got you to start writing down goals and solutions. I hope you stop all of this and get out of your hole before you dig deeper. I pray that this book finds you when you need it the most. Whether you're in a jail cell, divorced or broken up, lost your parents, bullied at school, or you feel like you just don't fit in, I pray this book motivates you. I pray a spark lands in you and bursts into a flame. Because no matter what you have done or what has happened to you, no one with a pure heart deserves to be alone.

Made in the USA
Columbia, SC
17 October 2022